The Quaker Way

Revised and updated by Friends General Conference
Religious Education Committee

from a 1958 publication of the Education Committee
of the General Meeting for Australia
of the Religious Society of Friends

illustrated by Signe Wilkinson

Published by Friends General Conference
ISBN 1-888305-06-1
© 1998 by Friends General Conference
Text may be freely reproduced with credit.

Illustrations © 1998 by Signe Wilkinson
  (1992 Pulitzer Prize-winning cartoonist for the
  Philadelphia Daily News, a.k.a. "attack Quaker")

Design and composition by David Budmen

For further information about this publication and other Quaker
resources, please contact:
Friends General Conference
1216 Arch Street, 2B
Philadelphia, PA 19107
www.fgcquaker.org

Special thanks to the following for their work on this project:

Beth Parrish	Nancy Moore
Marnie Clark	Liz Yeats

Contents

CHAPTER 1
The First Quakers

England was an exciting place in the 17th century. The first settlers had crossed the world to make their home in America, and sailors told of other lands only waiting for explorers to find them.

Similar discoveries were being made in the world of thought. People were finding new ideas—or old ones that had been forgotten. Ancient languages were found again, and a new language called "English" had grown up, expressing itself in plays and poetry. And now, in the early 17th century, came the King James Version English translation of the Bible which has meant so much to English speaking Christians ever since.

Men and women all over England were reading the Bible in their own language. They were asking questions about it. They wanted to learn all they could about religion and about God.

There was one group called "Seekers." They did not agree with the Christianity of their day. "The churches," they said, "have forgotten the real Christ. He lived a simple life. He could find God without candles and images." They wanted to return to the early Christianity where Christ's words and Christ's example were the things that mattered.

Living at that time was a young man named George Fox. He was a shoemaker and leatherworker in an English country town. He tells in his *Journal* how he struggled to find the truth, but for several years he was unhappy and uncertain.

Then one day, as he wrote later, "I heard a voice which said, 'There is one, even Christ Jesus, that can speak to your condition.'" And, George Fox goes on, "when I heard it, my heart did leap for joy." He felt within him "the greatness and infiniteness of the love of God."

He had rediscovered the truth which Jesus

brought sixteen hundred years before. There is, in each one of us, a small part of the spirit of God. It has many names. Some call it "the soul," "the spirit," "the seed of God," or "the Christ within." George Fox used the phrase, "that of God in every one." He also called it "the inner light"—the light of Christ that lights every person that comes into the world. Each one of us, because of that light within, can find God and speak to God without the help of a priest or minister.

That, said George Fox, was the most important fact in life. Religion wasn't just a matter of going to church, reading books about God, repeating prayers, or singing hymns, though these might be helpful. True religion was a personal experience. It was the spirit of God within us feeling the greater spirit of God outside ourselves. It was *knowing* God in our hearts.

When George Fox found this truth, he wanted to share it with others. So he travelled about England talking to people and holding meetings with them. Many of those he met with were from groups like the "Seekers." George Fox's message of "that of God in everyone" seemed right to them. They found they needed no minister and no special ceremonies. Women and men worshipped in silence. They tried to give their spirit to the spirit of God, and waited for God to tell them what to do and say. They became known as Children of Light, or the Friends of Truth, and later simply as Friends.

They needed friendship, because they had many enemies. They were attacked from every side—by those belonging to some Puritan groups and also by the Church of England. It is generally believed that the word "Quaker" was first used as a term of contempt.

Some Quakers went to America to start a new life in a new country. Most of them stayed in England to face ill-treatment and possible imprisonment. But the truth they found couldn't be stopped. They went on holding their meetings for worship; and in one place at least, when all the grown-ups were in prison, the children held the meeting by themselves.

At last, after a great deal of suffering, they were allowed to worship in their own way. Before George Fox died, in 1691, he saw "the people called Quakers" firmly established as a religious society in England and even in America, where he had traveled to share his ministry and spread his important discovery.

CHAPTER 2
Beliefs and Creeds

The Society of Friends does not have an official creed (or statement of beliefs) which all its members must accept. There are several reasons for this:

- Words often mean different things to different people.
- Words change their meanings. (That is why some parts of the Bible are now hard to understand.)
- God is always revealing new truths to us, or showing us truth in a new way. Truth cannot be explained forever in the same set of words.
- It isn't what we say about religion that matters so much as what we know about God in our hearts.

But putting our beliefs on paper can sometimes help us to see them more clearly—so long as we don't think they are final, or insist that everybody else agree with them. Talking it over among ourselves, or with family and other older Friends, may help us to understand more about Quakerism, and also help us to see our own beliefs more clearly. Remember: the *proof* of a belief lies in our own and others' experience of God, and the way we reflect and test it in our lives.

The following is an attempt that one Friend has made to put belief into words. Do not think of it as the opinion of the Society of Friends, but just as the thoughts of a single Friend that may set your own thoughts working:

- God is the great Spirit who made the universe and is still making it. God's work can be seen in everything that is beautiful and true and good.
- Each one of us has a part of God's own spirit. It helps us to see the beautiful, the true and the good in the world around us and in other people.

- Our spirit can unite with the greater spirit of God. We don't need a minister to do it for us. We don't need a particular set of words or ceremonies. We can find God through that part of the divine spirit—the inner light—which God has given to each of us.

- A part of the spirit which is in us is in every other man, woman and child in the world, whatever their race or religion.

- Some people—because they have followed the spirit within them more carefully, and given more time and thought to the search for truth—have come very close to God. Among them have been great teachers and healers such as Buddha, Isaiah, Mohammed, Julian of Norwich, Gandhi, and Mother Teresa. These spiritual leaders from all over the world had one thing in common: the inner light of the spirit burned so strongly in them that it lit a way to the truth, not only for themselves but for thousands of people who came after them.

- Many Friends believe the greatest of these teachers was Jesus of Nazareth. He was so close to God, so full of the divine spirit, that people said, "He must be the Son of God," and "There is God himself walking the earth as a man." (Mark 3:11) Thus, they called him Jesus Christ, or Jesus, the one sent by God. And Jesus himself told his disciples: "The Father and I are one." (John 10:30)

- Jesus wanted us to worship the God who sent him. ("Not I, but the Father who lives in me—he does the work.") Yet God's love and purpose are so clearly shown in the life and teachings of Jesus, that if we follow him, we also follow God.

Sometimes it is difficult for us to feel part of the great Spirit which made the universe. It seems too big for us to imagine. But Jesus, the carpenter's son, is always there as a magnificent example of God at work in this world.

This is only one Friend's statement of beliefs. Other Friends will express their beliefs in other ways. Talk to them, listen to them in meeting, study the Bible and other books, and gradually make up your own mind. If we really want understanding, we shall find it. For as Jesus said:

> Ask and it will be given to you;
> Search and you will find;
> Knock and the door will be opened.
>
> LUKE 11:9

CHAPTER 3

Because I Believe . . .

If we really believe in something, it is going to have an effect on our life. So let us consider this Friend's statement of belief point by point, and see what it means:

God is the great Spirit
who made the universe.

When we think of the world with all its beauty, and the millions of stars beyond, we are filled with wonder. We find it natural to worship the God who can create such marvellous things. To worship means "to love with wonder."

The chief commandment that Jesus gave us was: "Love God with all your heart, and with all your soul, and with all your strength, and with all your mind." (Mark 12:30) That, he said, is the most important thing in life.

If this is so, we must leave time in our lives to think of God. We must leave time to look at God's world where even the smallest leaf is beautiful.

We need to look for the enduring goodness of humankind, even when it's hard to see behind the headlines of the latest evil. Nature's beauty and human goodness can give us strength to help change the evil that does exist into good.

We must leave time for good books, good music and other great works of art, because these have been made by the spirit of God working through talented people. We must wonder at these things, use them to grow, and love and thank God who gave them to us.

We can thank God, too, for that beauty of order in the universe which is revealed to us by science. And we can use God's gifts of intelligence and curiosity to discover more and more of the wonders of creation.

Each one of us
has a part of God's own spirit.

As Jesus said, "The Kingdom of Heaven is within you." (Luke 17:21) This is a wonderful statement that needs a lot of thinking about.

Our spirit may be very small and weak at first—no larger, Jesus said, than the seed of a tiny plant. It grows if we care for it. But it lies dormant unless we value it and continually look after it.

It grows by thinking of whatever is beautiful and true and good:

> in the world which God made,
> in the lives of other people,
> in works of art.

And it grows still more when we try to grow what is true and good and beautiful in our own lives.

Our spirit can unite
with the greater spirit of God.

This can happen when we are by ourselves—if we give time for it. Jesus used to spend time in silence and prayer, sometimes in lonely places, so that he could feel God very close to him. We, too, need to be alone sometimes so that God can speak to us. As an awareness of God grows within us, we can find God anywhere—in the home, the classroom, or the busy street.

We are also helped by knowing that our beliefs are shared by other people. We help one another find God. That is why we have meeting for worship. By coming together and worshipping together we strengthen our beliefs. And because we are all at different stages of development, we can learn from one another. As Jesus promised:

> I shall be among any group of people who meet together in my name.
>
> MATTHEW 18:20

A part of the same spirit which is in us is in every man, woman and child.

We must love them because of this. They are children of the same loving God.

That was the second great commandment of Jesus, next in importance to loving God with all our heart, and with all our soul, and with all our strength, and with all our mind:

Love other people as much as you love yourselves.

MARK 12:31

That means we must try to help other people, not only in a practical way, but in their search for God.

Some people have lived close to God.

Such men and women have lived in every country, in every age, and there are still such people today. By studying their words and lives we can learn a great deal about their difficulties and how they overcame them, and share some of the truths they discovered. Among them are Isaiah, St. Theresa, St. Francis, John Woolman, Lucretia Mott, Gandhi, and Martin Luther King—to name only a few.

Many Friends believe the greatest of all was Jesus of Nazareth.

It is, of course, not only what Jesus said that matters, but how he lived. He is the great example of someone who did right and good. He worshipped God, and loved the things which God created. He valued the spirit of God in himself and in other people. He studied the lives and sayings of the Jewish prophets who lived before him. He was so much a part of God that when he spoke it was like God speaking. He told people the truth of God's love and power, and he healed their minds and bodies. He treated all people, even those who were disabled or thought to be doing immoral acts, with equal respect. In the end, he died for his beliefs, but he still lives on in spirit to help us. His example lives on.

By learning about Jesus we also learn about God. He said "Follow me," and it is by trying to follow his example, and learning to know him, that we learn to know God.

Jesus said:

I am the light of the world. No one who
follows me will walk in darkness.

JOHN 8:12

CHAPTER 4

Quaker Testimonies

Peace and War

Quakers are widely known as people who believe that war is wrong. Of course, we are not the only religious people who believe this, but we are respected for having believed it, as a group, for 300 years.

Our pacifism is not a separate belief. It is the result of our whole religion. If God is a spirit of love—creative, good and beautiful—how can that spirit want us to take part in something which is ugly, cruel and destructive? If other people are our friends, because, like us, they contain the spirit of God, how can we treat them as enemies and kill them?

Certain sayings of Jesus can be quoted to support our beliefs:

Blessed are those who make peace, because they shall be called the children of God.

MATTHEW 5:9

Those who take up the sword shall die by the sword.

MATTHEW 26:52

If my kingdom were of this world, then would my children fight?

JOHN 18:36

You have heard it said, "An eye for an eye, and a tooth for a tooth," but I say to you, Don't resist the man who wants to harm you . . .

MATTHEW 5:38–39

Love your enemies; do good to those who hate you; bless those who curse you, and pray for those who treat you badly.

LUKE 6:27–29

But words can be twisted or misunderstood. It is in the life and example of Jesus that we get the strength for our belief. Can we imagine him using a machine-gun or a flame-thrower, or dropping an atomic bomb? Can we imagine him wanting *us* to do so?

Those are the questions we have to answer. Beside them the justice or injustice of another cause doesn't matter. Our first loyalty is to the spirit of God, even though it may lead to suffering for ourselves and others.

We cannot believe that God intends us to do a violent or evil action in the hope that good may come of it. We still believe what the early Friends said to Charles II in 1660:

> We utterly deny all outward wars and strife, and fighting with outward weapons for any end, or under any pretence whatever; this is our testimony to the whole world. The Spirit of Christ by which we are guided is not changeable, so as once to command us from a thing as evil and again to move unto it; and we certainly know and testify to the world that the Spirit of Christ, which leads us into all Truth, will never move us to fight and war against any man with outward weapons, neither for the Kingdom of Christ nor for the kingdoms of this world.

This statement of the Society of Friends has never been bettered, but it has been repeated again and again since then by other Quakers:

> War and revenge are evils as opposite and contrary to the spirit and doctrine of Christ as light to darkness. . . . It is strange that men, made after the image of God, should have so much degenerated that they rather bear the image and nature of roaring lions, tearing tigers, devouring wolves and raging bears than of rational creatures endowed with reason.
>
> ROBERT BARCLAY (1678)

> A good end cannot sanctify evil means, nor must we do evil that good may come of it.
>
> WILLIAM PENN (1644–1718)

> War, all war, denies and re-crucifies our God. That is true, whether it is a defensive or aggressive war . . . and he who dares to subscribe to a Christian peace testimony can have no part or lot in any of it. This is and has been Friends' testimony to the whole world, to the whole Christian Church.
>
> *THE FRIEND*, NOVEMBER 9TH, 1956

Seek to 'live in the virtue of that life and power that takes away the occasion of all wars.'

War is contrary to the life and teaching of Jesus. Seek through God's power and grace to overcome in your hearts the emotions which lie at the root of conflict.

Every human being is a child of God, and has that divine spark which claims our reverence. War is a denial of this truth.

Friends' peace testimony is not negative. It is the positive exercise of good will calling us to lend our influence to all that strengthens the growth of international friendships and understanding.

Cultivate an active spirit of love and peace. Show a loving consideration for all creatures, cherishing the beauty and wonder of all God's creation. As parents and teachers, share this sense of reverence and stewardship.

PEACE AND NONVIOLENCE
SOUTHEASTERN YEARLY MEETING, 1987

Peace is the state in which we are in accord with God, the Earth, others and ourselves. We know that truth, lasting peace among us can finally be attained only through unity in the life of the spirit. We work to create the conditions of peace, such as freedom, justice, cooperation, and the right sharing of the world's resources.

As we work for peace in the world, we search out the seeds of war in ourselves and in our way of life. We refuse to join in actions which lead to destruction and death. We seek ways to cooperate to save life and strengthen the bonds of unity among all people.

PEACE, NORTH PACIFIC YEARLY MEETING, 1993

Most Friends refuse to join the army, navy, or air force, or take any part in preparations for war. They will do something constructive to help those in need, but they will not take part in destruction. Some have performed alternative service in hospitals, worked for the American Friends Service Committee, or done other social service work. Some have worked on the land. Others have gone to prison because they believe that it is helping the war to do any work under orders from the State in wartime.

Each of us has to decide how far to go. We can ask our family and others in our meeting to help us decide by forming a group to seek clearness. Sitting together in silence waiting upon God, we can often discover the best action to take.

The following points are worth discussing:

1. Think about the causes of war. One country may be afraid of another. Nations may dislike each other because of something that happened in the past. One may be jealous of another, or want more land or more trade. There are many different causes. Can we find out what these are, and prevent them from leading to war? Just as each of us is trying to have respect and goodwill towards other people, so, as a country, we should behave to other nations.

2. It is no use opposing great wars if there are small ones in our own lives. If we quarrel with other people and bear them

grudges, we are creating a state of war around us. We must try, as George Fox said, "to live in the life and power that takes away the occasion of all wars."

3. Refusal to take part in war does not mean that we can ignore evil, or pretend that it doesn't exist. Jesus was always denouncing wrongs and injustices. But he attacked evil with the inward weapon of the spirit. Can this spirit grow within us, so that we have something positive to offer in place of war?

Service and Friendship

"Is the work I am doing, or intend to do when I leave school, the work that God wants me to do?" That is a question that every young Friend should ask. What we do in our spare time is important, but what we do in our chosen career is more important still. We must try to develop, as far as we can, the special abilities that God has given us, and use these in our work.

If this question is too hard to answer at present, we can ask this question: Is the work going to help other people? Is it contributing something to the world's peace or knowledge or happiness? Or is it simply a way of making money?

Friends have always felt that our work should be the outward expression of our belief. It is no good having a religion for Sundays only. It should be there seven days a week. In fact, when others think of us, they remember people like Elizabeth Fry, who worked in prisons; John Woolman, who helped to end slavery; Lucretia Mott, who worked for abolition and women's rights; William Tuke, who started the first mental hospital in England; Maria Mitchell, America's first woman astronomer; Alice Paul, leader in the American suffrage movement; Thomas Story, in geology, the study of rocks; Bayard Rustin, Civil Rights organizer; and Kathleen Lonsdale, the nuclear scientist. But there have been many others who have helped in less noticeable ways—for instance, by being honest shopkeepers, who put a fair price on their goods instead of bargaining over them, or caring nurses, who attend those with AIDS.

There are many ways in which we can be of service to God through our work. We can help the building of the world as workers and crafts people. We can help people's bodies as doctors, nurses and relief workers. We can help their minds as teachers, lecturers and scientists. We can help their spirits and imagination as writers, musicians and artists. One way is not necessarily better than another. Each of us is different, and has different gifts to offer.

And our age doesn't matter. Jesus was young when he started his work. So were George Fox and Lucretia Mott. So were Mozart, Emily Dickinson, and many others whose works are remembered today.

Jesus' words, "Love your neighbor as yourself" (Luke 10:30–37) are not easy ones to follow. In his story of the Good Samaritan he shows us that "neighbor" means not only the person living next door or in the same town or country. All people are our neighbors because they live in the same world. All people are our brothers and sisters because they share the same Light within.

Women and Men

Jesus treated men and women as equals. We are all different, and have different gifts to offer the world, but we believe that one gender is not better than another. Women and men have an equal share in our meetings for worship, and in business meetings.

Discrimination

Quakers have believed that all people, rich and poor, are equal before God. The color of one's skin, whether black, white, brown or yellow, doesn't matter. What does matter is the spirit under the skin. That is why Quakers were among the first to speak and act against slavery. No race has the right to make another race its servants. Today we are opposed to racism, class discrimination and oppressive treatment of people anywhere.

Politics and Religion

Quakers also have believed in political and religious freedom. No group of people, we think, should be able to force its beliefs on to another group. Everyone should be empowered to think and worship freely.

We have always worked for this tolerance — for ourselves and for others. Even if we believe that our way of thinking is the right way, no good can come of forcing other people to agree. We can try to persuade them but they must accept willingly from their own spirit.

Betting and Gambling

Friends are opposed to betting and gambling. We believe that the desire to get money without working for it can destroy our sense of true values. We believe also that the spirit of adventure can be satisfied in better ways.

Alcohol, Drugs, Tobacco

Friends know the harm to health, unhappiness and waste of money that can come from the abusive consumption of addictive substances, such as alcohol, drugs and tobacco. We don't insist that members abstain completely from these substances, but we do ask them to consider this question: "Might it be better for my own health and as an example to others, to abstain from alcohol, drugs and tobacco?"

Abstaining from the use of alcohol is one of the more recent ideas of the Society. In the early days there were several Quaker firms producing beer, but by the early 19th century it was felt that this was not a helpful way of earning a living, and Friends turned their attention to producing other products.

Oaths

Jesus said, "Let your 'yes' mean yes and your 'no' mean no." (Matthew 5:37) Quakers have always been against the taking of oaths. We do not think that there should be two standards of truth—one for everyday life and one for the court of law. We should speak the truth wherever we are.

Their refusal to take oaths sent many early Friends to prison, but now we are allowed to "affirm" in court. They say, "I _____, do solemnly, sincerely and truly declare and affirm that . . ." We do not have to "swear on the Bible."

When considering how we implement these testimonies among Friends these words of Jesus (based on J. B. Phillips' translation) are worth remembering:

> Don't judge other people, and you will not be judged. Don't condemn them, and you will not be condemned. Make allowances for others, and they will make allowances for you. Give, and others will give to you.
> MATTHEW 7:1–2

> Treat people exactly as you would like them to treat you.
> MATTHEW 7:12

> This I command you, that you love one another.
> JOHN 15:12–17

And this saying from Jesus the carpenter, which shows his sense of humor:

> Don't complain about the speck of sawdust in someone else's eye, when there is a whole plank in your own!
>
> MATTHEW 7:3–5

CHAPTER 5
Meeting for Worship

THE meeting for worship is the center of Quaker life. At any time during the week we can worship alone. On Sundays we meet to worship with others, sitting in silence, seeking to find God together.

Unprogrammed Friends meet in silence, because we don't want anything to distract us while we are trying to come close to God. There are two ways of doing this. We can think of our spirit reaching out toward God. Or we can think that we are opening our minds and hearts so that God can come to us. Whichever way we look at it, the important thing is that, in the silence of meeting, our spirit may meet God's spirit.

There are no set words or ceremonies in unprogrammed meetings. All those present may be moved to speak their own service.

Talk about semi-programed mtg.

We are asked by the Advices to come "with heart and mind prepared." We wait for God to tell us what to do. If he wants us to speak, we believe that he will also give us the words to say. One person may offer a prayer, another may read from the Bible, a third may give a message that has come during the meeting or has grown out of past experience or study. Sometimes nothing is said during the whole meeting. This doesn't matter as long as we have found God in the silence.

Some young people find this waiting difficult. Some adults also find it difficult. Our meetings for worship have no outside aids, such as an elaborate building, music or ritual. We have to find the way ourselves, and the way is different every Sunday. Sometimes, it is hard work. In fact, Quaker worship is an art; and like every art it means continual practice—trying, failing and trying again, before we are successful. And, as with every other art, we never finish learning.

Some people new to silent worship have found these suggestions helpful. Trying one or two of them each meeting can help you find your own most comfortable way of opening up to God:

[handwritten note: Kids - go around & each read one.]

- Come into meeting quietly. Remember that you are coming together to join with others in thought, prayer and thanksgiving.
- Imagine you are sitting in some quiet, beautiful part of God's creation.
- Thank God for the world, and for the people in it.
- Tell God the things that are worrying you, and lose them in the silence.
- Bring to the meeting thoughts you have been pondering and release them into the silence.
- Remember some words of Jesus and think about them.
- See, in your imagination, some happening in the life of Jesus. Watch him healing someone. Hear him telling a parable as if you were one of his listeners.
- Ask God for greater love and understanding.
- Keeping your mind and body still, let your spirit reach out toward the spirit of God.

- When your thoughts wander, don't worry. Draw them back quietly and happily.
- If you leave before the meeting is over, go quietly. Remember that other Friends are still waiting on God. You don't want to disturb them.
- It is good to remember it is not only those who speak in meeting who help others. Our feelings can be shared without any words being spoken. Young people can help in this way as well as grown-ups.

operator assisted   direct-dial Party Line

CHAPTER 6

How and Why Are Quakers Different from Other Faith Communities?

This question is often asked by children of Quaker families, and by those outside the Society. Here are some answers to think about and discuss.

Why do we worship in plain buildings?

A special building is not necessary for worshipping God. Friends have said: "Give us the barest of rooms and we can worship God anywhere." But although we haven't built any large and beautiful churches like the English cathedrals, our meeting houses have often been simple and beautiful—just as plain well-made furniture has a beauty of its own. This is particularly true of meetinghouses that were built in England and America during the 18th century. New meetinghouses in the future could have the same simple beauty.

Why don't unprogrammed Friends have a priest or minister?

Some Friends in the United States and other parts of the world do have a paid minister, but this is unusual in unprogrammed meetings. Most Friends have believed that religion is something between God and each individual. We can each find God without a paid minister to help us. But this doesn't mean that we don't have ministers in our meeting for worship. It means that each one of us is a minister. We all have a part to play in a successful meeting for worship.

Why aren't children christened or baptized?

We believe, as one Friend has said, that every child, as soon as he is born, becomes a member of God's family. No ceremony is needed.

Why don't we have the communion service?

We do have communion. The whole aim of a meeting for worship is communion (or uniting) with God. But we don't feel that outward sacraments are necessary. All life— all the week—should be a kind of sacrament. That is, we should always act knowing that God is present to us.

Why isn't there an altar?

We do not believe that an altar is necessary for worship. (Early Friends would probably have added that altars were pagan in origin.)

Why aren't hymns and music used in our meetings for worship?

Hymns would have to be chosen and prepared beforehand, and that is difficult with a form of worship which waits for God to lead it. However, many Friends enjoy music and many meetings sing regularly before or after worship and at social occasions. Sometimes the vocal ministry of an individual Friend will include singing during worship. Others who feel moved may join in the singing.

What is a Quaker marriage?

We believe that God alone can join two people together in marriage, so no priest or church official is needed. Also, from the beginning, marriage of a woman and man in a Quaker meeting has been the joining of two equal human beings who have the same rights and privileges within the marriage. The marriage between Margaret Fell and George Fox was a good example of such a marriage. Although in other religious traditions marriage has signified the woman becoming the property of the man, this has never been the case among Friends.

When two Friends request to marry under the care of the Meeting, a clearness committee helps them make sure they are ready. An oversight committee helps the couple plan the marriage and meet the legal requirements.

The wedding begins with silent meeting for worship. After a time the couple rise, hold hands, and promise with Divine assistance to be loving and faithful to each other. After the couple signs the marriage certificate, a Friend reads it aloud. Meeting for worship continues; any may speak as she or he is moved. At the close of meeting, those present are asked to sign the certificate as witnesses.

People belonging to other churches may not agree with all these ideas. They find that ceremonies are helpful in bringing them closer to God. No single type of religion need be right for everyone. We have simply chosen what seems right for us, believing that, if we have been sincere, God will overlook mistakes and show us a better way.

At the same time, we should try to understand more about other forms of religion.

That is why we support the World Council of Churches and other ecumenical and interfaith organizations where men and women of various religions can meet together for discussion. Then we discover that, although we disagree on some points, there are very many on which we agree.

While many Friends believe that in Jesus God is most clearly revealed and that Jesus is the best guide to living, we also know that there are many paths to God. Many men and women of other religions—Islam, Judaism, Hinduism, Budhism, to name a few—have known God and lived good lives.

So let us keep our beliefs, while respecting the beliefs of others. And let us learn what they have to teach us. Understanding their religions will also help us to understand the people themselves—their true selves—and that is essential if we are to work with them and to live in peace together.

CHAPTER 7
How the Society Works

George Fox was a practical man as well as a religious one. He saw the dangers which the Society would face after he died. With no creed, no paid minister and no regular service, it could have become a series of separate meetings and died out. It needed an organization of some kind to hold it together. So George Fox with the help of other early Friends, especially Margaret Fell, began to develop one. Much of the original structure, tested by time and leadings from God, still exists today.

In North America, today, each local meeting is a monthly meeting. Besides the meeting for worship, it holds a regular, monthly meeting for worship for business which all members are expected to attend. Some monthly meetings have worship groups or preparative meetings under their care. Worship groups and preparative meetings hold regular meetings for worship but members participate in the meeting for business of the monthly meeting that has care of the group.

Monthly meeting makes most of the important decisions concerning Friends' work—money, the meetinghouse itself, and the admission of new members. Much of the work in each monthly meeting is done by committees. Most meetings have some of the following committees:

Ministry and Worship has care of the meeting for worship and the spiritual life of the meeting as a whole and its individual members and attenders.

Oversight has responsibility for the pastoral care of members and attenders, usually including marriages, membership and visiting the ill.

Nominating finds members of the meeting to serve as officers: clerk, recording clerk and treasurer, and on committees.

Religious Education provides learning opportunities for members and attenders of all ages.

Property Committee cares for the meeting-house and area around it, sometimes including a graveyard.

Peace and Social Concerns coordinates the social concerns work of the meeting, often including working with local shelters, concern for the environment, and work for peace and justice.

Your meeting may have other committees for special purposes, including a committee to supervise a school, reach out to Quakers known in the community, or work on a special short-term project.

In many places there are quarterly meetings, made up of several monthly meetings, which meet four times a year to discuss anything that is of importance to them all.

Next there are yearly meetings. In North America these are regional, bringing together and helping nurture many different monthly meetings.

Next there are very large national Quaker bodies like Friends General Conference and Friends United Meeting that offer services to help yearly meetings and, through them, to help individual Friends like the ones in your own meeting.

At all these levels there are specific committees to carry out the work. Though organizational details differ in different parts of the world where there are Quakers, the concept is the same—each member has a responsibility in the practical working of the Society. Business is not left to a "church council," minister or denominational officer. We are all expected to play our part by serving on committees at all levels. In this way, with an organization that is regular but not too rigid, the Society of Friends has survived for over 300 years.

The World Family of Friends

To give Friends all over the world a sense of belonging together, there is a Friends World Committee for Consultation. The Committee arranges conferences in various parts of the world. These are usually for one region, like Europe or North America, but occasionally for all Friends.

Membership

In some meetings if a child is born into a Quaker family, the meeting may consider that child a "birthright member" needing no special separate membership process. In others, the parents may register the child as an associate or junior member of the Society of Friends. The young person may apply for adult membership when he or she is ready.

Someone not brought up as a Quaker usually becomes a member more gradually. He or she begins by coming to meeting for worship. People who come regularly are known as attenders. Later they may apply for membership by writing to the local clerk. The letter is read at the next monthly meeting, or referred to the appropriate committee. Friends are appointed to visit and talk with the attender. They report to the next meeting, where the application is considered and usually accepted.

QUERY 20. GOOD TASTE.

Does your Meeting strive to carry out all functions in good taste?

Do meeting furnishings reflect quiet elegance, no matter the cost?

Do members take care to own only wood furniture?

Preferably antiques. Preferably inherited?

Do members try to eliminate all synthetics from their wardrobes?

Is simplicity extended to all our possessions — eliminating all chrome and fins from our Volvos?

Just as our mighty oak spreads its leaves in God's wonderful sense of design, so, too, should Friends order our lives in good taste and....

CHAPTER 8
Advices and Queries

"Advices and Queries" for grown-ups are sometimes read in meeting. Some Friends have drawn up the following suggestions for young people but you should also check the Faith and Practice of your yearly meeting for other advices and queries:

Advices

- Feel God near you all day long.
- Listen to God's voice in your heart.

- Try to live close to Jesus every day.
- Remember his words and try to follow them.
- Study his life, and think how your own life can be changed by him.

- Be kind to other people. Don't quarrel or say spiteful things.
- Forgive people when they say or do anything that hurts you.
- Be friendly to people. Do all you can to help them.

- Be kind to animals and birds, which are also God's creatures.
- Respect the trees and flowers God has created. Do not destroy anything unnecessarily.

- Be sincere. Find your true self, and act from it.
- Be honest in thought, word and deed.
- Be tolerant. Hold to your belief, but keep your mind open to new light.
- Read and talk so as to find out further truth and greater understanding.
- Take care of your body. It is the home of your spirit.

Queries

- Do you leave time in the day to be with God, and let God speak to you?
- Do you go to Meeting as often as you can? Do you prepare yourself for it?
- Do you study the life and teachings of Jesus as told in the Bible, and do you try to follow him?

- Are you looking for what is true and good and beautiful in all things?
- Are you careful in choosing your clothes, books, films, music and television programs?
- Will humankind be helped in body, mind or spirit by the work you do in life?

- Do you always try to tell the truth?
- Are you honest with money, and fair in sport?

- Do you respect the spirit of God in others?
- Are you courteous to everyone under all conditions?

- Do you treat others as you'd like to be treated yourself?
- Do you try to work well and cheerfully at home and at school?
- Do you take your share of responsibility at Young Friends' meetings and in your home?

- Do you stand out against actions that you believe to be wrong?
- Do you keep your courage even when you are afraid?

- Do you forgive those who have said and done things that hurt you?
- If others quarrel, do you try to make peace between them?
- Do you think of those less fortunate than yourself and try to help them?

THE LAST PHILADELPHIA QUAKER

CHAPTER 9
Prayer

Praying means talking to God. It also means learning to listen to God and learning to hold yourself open to God's direction.

The best prayers are those we make up ourselves. Someone else's prayer may sometimes serve as a model, but we need to remember Christ' warning when he gave us "The Lord's Prayer" as a model: "Don't repeat meaningless words."

These are just a few of the prayers which children and grown-ups have sent us. The Advices and Queries on pages 57 to 60 may help you to make up others.

The Lord's Prayer
Our Father, which art in heaven:
Great Spirit, parent of us all:

Hallowed be thy name:
  May we love and praise you.
Thy Kingdom come,
  May the world become a just and peaceful
  place.
Thy will be done, on earth as it is in heaven.
  May your desires be carried out on earth.
*And forgive us our trespasses, as we forgive
  them that trespass against us*:
  Forgive us the wrongs we do to you, in the
  same way as we forgive the wrongs done
  to us by other people.
*Lead us not into temptation, but deliver us
  from evil*.
  We hope that we will not be tempted;
  but if we are tempted, help us to choose
  the right way.
*For thine is the kingdom, the power and the
  glory, forever and ever*.
  For the kingdom of the Spirit is yours, and you
  have power over everything, now and always.
                    MATTHEW 6:9–13

God be in my head, and in my understanding;
God be in my eyes, and in my looking;

God be in my mouth, and in my speaking;
God be in my heart, and in my thinking;
God be at my end, and at my departing.

May the strength of God pilot us;
May the power of God preserve us;
May the wisdom of God instruct us;
May the hand of God protect us. . . .
ST. PATRICK'S BREASTPLATE

Of Thee three things we pray:
To know Thee more clearly,
Love Thee more dearly,
Follow Thee more nearly,
Day by day.

We thank you, O God, for the sunlight,
    and all that lives on the earth.
We thank you for the friends who enjoy it
    with us,
We ask you to remember those who, for
    any reason, are unable to enjoy it.

Help us, God, to love other people, and keep us unhurt and unresentful if they cannot return our love. Knowing that we live in the light of your love, what have we to fear?

For our bodies, strongly and wonderfully made,
    We give thanks.
For our minds, delicate and willing,
    We give thanks.
For our spirits, through which the holy Spirit
    of God may move in us,
    We give thanks.

Oh God, help us:
to think what is fine,
to do what is kind,
to say what is true.

Every day, God, we have decisions to make.
Give us wisdom to choose always the right.

God of Truth, we pray for all the people of the world, that each person will search for truth within and, finding it, will recognize it in other people.

Great Spirit of Light: we pray for light—for always, like the flowers of the trees, we turn toward it. In this light, O God, we know that we shall choose the true way of life.

Let Your great silence fold me round
Until, through every lovely sound
Of music, birds, of wind and sea,
I hear Your kind voice speak to me.

Teach me to listen, Lord.
Teach me to catch the voice of heaven in earthly things.
Equip me with antennae to pick up and select, out of the cacophony

that drums against my ear,
your voice.
Amplify in my ear truth-sounds.

Teach me to listen, too,
with hands and feet,
translating your voice
into my daily walk and way.
Teach me to listen. (Robin E. Van Cleef)

Lord, make me an instrument of thy peace.
Where there is hatred, let me show love;
Where there is injury, pardon;
Where there is doubt, faith;
Where there is darkness, light;
Where there is sadness, joy.

O, Divine Master, grant that I may not so
much seek to be consoled, as to console;
to be understood, as to understand;
to be loved, as to love;
for it is in giving that we receive;
it is in pardoning that we are pardoned;
and it is in dying that we are born to
eternal life.

ST. FRANCIS OF ASSISI

CHAPTER 10

First Day School

An hour is a long time for the younger children to sit in meeting for worship. So they usually come into the ordinary meeting for a short period, and spend the rest of the time at a meeting of their own, or in First Day School, learning something about Quaker ways.

This period may be spent in saying prayers, singing hymns, listening to stories or music or drawing pictures. Young people also learn about God and Jesus and the lives of men and women who have followed God's teachings. There are periods of silence to learn how to be in meeting for worship later on.

During First Day School there are sometimes lessons from the Bible, which is a collection of great religious books written by poets, story-tellers and prophets who lived many years ago. It can teach us a great deal about how our religion grew and give us ideas to think about. The most important part to us, as Christians, is the New Testament, because it tells us the life of Jesus.

We also read from other books, in prose and poetry. Some young people like to collect these extracts and make a book of their own. Here are a few collected with the help of young people:

> I expect to pass through this world but once;
>   Any good thing, therefore that I can do,
> Or any kindness that I can show to any
>   fellow-creature,
> Let me do it now; let me not defer or neglect it,
> For I shall not pass this way again.

> Whatsoever things are true,
> Whatsoever things are honest,
> Whatsoever things are pure,
> Whatsoever things are lovely,
> Whatsoever things are of good report—think of these things.
>
> St. Paul (Philippians 4:8)

Open your eyes, and the whole world is full of God.

JACOB BOEHME

Is goodness really far off? I long for goodness, and look!—goodness is at hand.

The person who knows the truth isn't equal to the person who loves it.

Do not do to others what you would not like yourself.

THREE SAYINGS OF CONFUCIUS

The Serenity Prayer

God, grant me the serenity
to accept the things I cannot change,
the courage to change the things I can,
and the wisdom to know the difference.

Let a person overcome anger by love; overcome evil by good; overcome the greedy by generosity; overcome the liar by truth.

THE BUDDHA

The most precious thing . . . is gentleness. . . . The greatest conquerors are those who overcome their enemies without strife.

LAO TZE

Let there be peace on earth—and let it begin with me.

AUTHOR UNKNOWN

Christ has no body now on earth but yours; no hands but yours, no feet but yours. Yours are the eyes through which is to look out Christ's compassion to the world; yours are the feet on which God is to go about doing good; and yours are the hands with which God is to bless us now.

ST. TERESA

Faith is the bird that feels the light and sings when the dawn is still dark.

RABINDRANATH TAGORE

Be still, and know that I am God.

PSALM 46

Drop Thy still dews of quietness
Till all our strivings cease.
Take from our souls the strain and stress
And let our ordered lives confess
The beauty of Thy peace.   J. G. WHITTIER

God is neither Catholic nor Protestant, neither Moslem nor Hindu. God is too great to be imprisoned in a single creed.

AUTHOR UNKNOWN

CHAPTER 11
Quaker Words

"Inner Light" or "Inward Light"

It is hard to describe this "something of God" which is in each one of us. It cannot be seen or heard. It can only be felt. Some people call it "the Spirit." To George Fox it was "the inner light"—"inner" because it is inside us, and "light" because it helps us to see things more clearly.

"With heart and mind prepared"

It is suggested that everyone coming to meeting for worship should come "with heart and mind prepared." This means having heart and mind ready to worship. It does not mean coming with words prepared beforehand to read or to say. The Quaker form of worship depends on our "waiting for God."

"Centering down"

The beginning of a meeting for worship is not always silent. There may be shuffling or someone coming in late. And when everything is quiet and our bodies are still, there is usually another period when our minds are restless. We are thinking of many different things connected with our everyday lives. Then we try to center our thoughts on God. When the meeting has succeeded in doing this, we say it has "centered down."

"A gathered meeting"

When a meeting for worship has centered down, God is able to speak to each of us in our hearts. Then, if we continue to center our thought on God, the whole meeting may find itself drawn together, as if we were all thinking and feeling as one. We call this a "gathered meeting," because God has gathered or united us. It is an experience we all hope for, but cannot always achieve.

"Message"

During the silence of a meeting for worship, each of us tries to hear the voice of God. Sometimes when God has spoken to us, we feel led to share through words with others, so we stand up and speak. What we say then is sometimes called "a message."

"Vocal ministry"

In most churches one person is appointed as minister. He or she decides the order of service, selects the prayers and hymns, and delivers a sermon. There is no such minister in our meeting. Instead, we are all ministers. Every one of us has a responsibility and shares in the ministry. We each, by our thoughts, decide how the meeting will go. We can help in this way without giving a spoken prayer or message, but when we do feel it right to speak, this is called "vocal ministry."

"Birthright members"

This term is not often used nowadays. It referred to Friends born of Quaker families registered as Quakers at birth. Friends admitted to Quakerism later in life were known as "convinced Friends."

"The sense of the meeting"

No votes are taken in our business meetings. Instead, the clerk listens to each speaker and then experience "the sense of the meeting." If there is disagreement, the clerk may call for a period of silence, so that members can bring the matter before God. If there is still disagreement, nothing is decided and the subject is brought up again at the next meeting. In this way we try to arrive at a decision which is accepted by the meeting as a whole.

"Concern"

Sometimes we feel that God has a special piece of work for us to do. It is then said that we "have a concern" to do it. John Woolman had a concern to help those suffering from slavery.

"Book of Discipline"

This is a book containing extracts from Quaker writings during the last 350 years, so that Friends can read about what Friends believed and learn from them. It also may contain queries and advices and procedures for carrying out the business of the Society. Many Friends in North America call these books "Faith and Practice." The book you are reading is a kind of "Young People's Book of Discipline."

"Elders and Overseers"

Elders are responsible for the proper conduct of the meeting, and the religious education of members. In the late 20th century many meetings no longer appoint Elders but give the same responsibilities to a committee, usually called Ministry and Worship.

Overseers are concerned for the personal welfare of members. In most monthly meetings, Overseers form a committee and may be responsible for marriages, membership and memorial services.

"Epistle"

At each yearly meeting a few Friends are asked to put the thoughts of the meeting into words. The clerk reads this "epistle" (an old word for letter) and after any alterations which are made by the whole meeting, it is sent out to other meetings so that the experience of the yearly meeting may be shared with Friends everywhere.

"Quakers"

We are not quite sure how this word began. It may have come from early Friends who "quaked at the word of the Lord." It may have come from certain members who, in the excitement of speaking in meeting, were seen to quake and tremble. If it was first used mockingly by other people, Friends have "lived it down" and it is no longer a term of contempt.

"Quaker Dress"

The first Friends dressed in the simplest fashion of their day as they felt outward appearance was much less important than inward faith. Later Friends kept this costume—and so defeated the original aim and became "special" and "different." It wasn't until the 19th century that Friends began to dress again in the style of their own time. Nowadays we still try to dress as simply as we can in clothes that are sturdy, easy to care for and often aesthetically pleasing.

"First Day" and "First Month"

Early Friends did not like the names of the days and months because these were pagan in origin. Thursday, for instance, came from Thor, the pagan god of thunder; August was named after a Roman Emperor, Augustus. So they referred to the days and months by number. They said, "a meeting will be held on First Day" or "yearly meeting will be in Fifth Month." These expressions are still used by a few of the older Friends but the practice is dying out.

"Thee" and "Thou"

In the 17th century, "thee" was used when speaking to people of your class or below, and "you" to those of classes above you. Friends believed that all people were equal, so they used "thee" or "thou" to everyone. Nowadays, of course, "you" is general, and there is no need for us to use any other words.

Christian names and Surnames

For the same reason, early Friends did not call certain people "Mister" or "Master." They thought that titles of all kinds hid the fact that people were equal before God. They therefore referred to each other as plain "George Fox" or "Margaret Fell." The practice continues today.

BIBLIOGRAPHY
Some Books to Read

The main source of authority for Friends is the Inner Light, the Living Christ, the eternal teacher. The Bible is an important secondary source.

There are two parts to the Bible. The older, generally called the Old Testament, contains books about Jewish history, laws, songs and instructions for living. The stories show how people related to God. This is the Bible that Jesus grew up with and learned and taught from during his life.

The newer one, called the New Testament, was written by men who knew Jesus as a man, or heard about him from his friends. It tells us all we know about the things Jesus did and the words he spoke, and about the early Christians (followers of Jesus) sharing the message. From the Bible we can discover how Christianity grew out of the Jewish religion.

There are many English translations of the Bible. For beautiful language and to use the one used by early Quakers, Friends may choose the King James version. However, its meaning is not always easy to follow because it was translated in the 17th century. Some prefer to use modern translations which are easier to understand, including the New Revised Standard Version and the Good News Bible. Each has its advantages and is worth exploring.

Some more books that share the workings of the Spirit include:

The Bible

*Graystone, Peter, illus. by Jacqui Thomas. *If I Had Lived in Jesus' Time*. Abingdon, 1995. 32 pp. Colorfully illustrated book designed to help children understand Jesus' time.

*Hastings, Selina, illus. by Eric Hastings. *The Children's Illustrated Bible*. Dorling Kindersley Limited, 1994. 320 pp. Richly illustrated bible for young children through elementary ages.

*Available through the FGC Bookstore.

Jones, Jessie Orton. *Small Rain: Verses from the Bible*. New York: The Viking Press, 1944 (OP available from Philadelphia YM Library). Assorted verses from the Bible. Two-color drawings. Older book.

*NIV *Young Discoverers Bible*. Zondervan, 1985. 1970 pp. Large type, written in accessible language with occasional pictures, a perfect children's Bible.

*Sasso, Sandy Eisenberg, illus. by Bethanne Anderson. *But God Remembered: Stories of Women from Creation to the Promised Land*. Jewish Lights, 1995. 31 pp. Stories that celebrate courageous and wise women from ancient tradition.

*Sasso, Sandy Eisenberg. *Prayer for the Earth: The Story of Naamah, Noah's Wife*. Jewish Lights, 1996. 32 pp. Illustrated story full of Naamah's wisdom and love for the natural harmony of the earth.

📖*Spears, Joanne and Larry. *Friendly Bible Study*. Philadelphia: Friends General Conference, 1990. 18 pp. Bible study method for small groups, with instructions for using this method with young people.

Worship

Baylor, Byrd. *Everybody Needs a Rock*. New York: Aladden, 1974. Idea for heightening awareness of surroundings for beginning stages for meditation.

*Baylor, Byrd. *The Other Way to Listen*. Scribner. Illustrated classic on learning to listen to the world around us.

📖Adult book but accessible to good readers.

Baylor, Byrd. *When Clay Sings*. New York: Chas Scribner's Sons, 1972. Native American pottery, it is believed, has a spirit—a voice of its own. The author is sensitive to the sound of that small voice.

📖*Havens, Teresina. *Mind What Stirs in Your Heart*. Pendle Hill Pamphlet 304, 1992. 40 pp. Taps into the deep flowing source, inviting each of us to enter into its silence and simplicity. Exercises to help us find our own connections through breathing, walking, and waiting.

Keats, Ezra Jack. *God is in the Mountains*. New York, 1966. A book that shows the many forms God takes in the beliefs of diverse peoples and their religions.

📖Lawrence, Brother. *The Practice of the Presence of God* (in many formats from different publishers). Classic devotional piece on daily living in God's presence.

LeTord, Bijou. *Peace on Earth: A Book of Prayers from Around the World*. Doubleday, 1992. 88 pp. Beautifully illustrated celebration of creation. Prayers are drawn from a multicultural set of spiritual traditions.

Progoff, Ira. *The Well and the Cathedral: An Entrance to Meditation*. Dialogue House Library, 1985. Format for older children.

About God

*Boritzer, Etan. *What is God?* Firefly. An illustrated children's book that tackles a big question: What God might be, how God might feel, what people long ago though God was. Perspectives from Judaism, Christianity, Moslem, and Buddhism.

Doane, Pelagie. *God Made the World*. Philadelphia: A.B. Lippincott, 1960. An older book for young children which talks about finding God all around us.

*Fager, Chuck. *Why God Is Like a Wet Bar of Soap*. Kimo, 1992. 18 pp. A father's poignant, often funny, and informative answer to his child's questions about God.

*Kroll, Virginia, illus. by Debra Reid Jenkins. *I Wanted to Know All About God*. Eerdmans, 1994. Engaging book invites children to experience God in their daily lives. Richly illustrated.

*Probasco, Teri, illus. by Margaret Brace. *Edge of the Night Sky*. Philadelphia: Friends General Conference, 1995. 32 pp. Inspiring naration and rich illustrations tell the story of a young child's experience of God's presence late at night in a cold barn while helping nurture new-born lambs.

*Sasso, Sandy E., illustrator. *God's Paintbrush*. Jewish Lights, 1992. 32 pp. Colorful multicultural, multiracial book about God from a young child's viewpoint.

*Stone, Phoebe, illus. by Sandy Eisenberg Sasso. *In God's Name*. Jewish Lights, 1994. 32 pp. Modern brightly illustrated fable about the search for God's name. This children's book celebrates the diversity and unity of all the people of the world.

*Sweetland, Nancy, illus. by Rick Stevens. *God's Quiet Things*. Eerdmans, 1994. 30 pp. Delightful lyrics and rich pastel illustrations reveal to children the wondrous quiet pieces of God's creation.

Walcott. *I Can See What God Does*. Nashville: Abingdon

Press, 1969. An older book that explains one sees God through other happenings and people in our world.

*Wood, Douglas, illus. by Cheng-Khee Chee. *Old Turtle*. Pfeifer-Hamilton, 1992. Full of wisdom and beautiful pictures, this book challenges children of all ages to think about God, our responsibility to the earth, and to the creatures on it.

Quakerism

*Briggs, Elinor, Marrie Clark, Carol Passmore, eds. *Lighting Candles In The Dark*. Friends General Conference, 1991. Stories with many uses. For the joy of family reading or as a meditation piece.

Brinton, Margaret, McWhirter, and Schroeder. *Candles in the Dark*, Friends General Conference, 1968. The old version of the stories. Many meeting libraries have this.

Broomall, Ayra, Pettit. *Friendly Story Caravan*. Pendle Hill, 1962. rev. ed., 1990. Quaker anthology of stories illustrating God's power in the life experience or ordinary people. Good for family reading or use with First Day School.

📖*Cooper, Wilmer. *A Living Faith: An Historical Study of Quaker Beliefs*. Friends United Press, 1990. 217 pp. Account of changing Quaker belief. Excellent background for discussing contemporary Friends theology.

📖Cooper, Wilmer. *The Testimony of Integrity in the Religious Society of Friends*. Pendle Hill Pamphlet #296, 1991. 31 pp. A call for us to model lives of integrity. Might be good basis for discussion with a teen or adult First Day School class.

📖*Cope-Robinson, Lyn. *The Little Quaker Sociology Book.* Canmore, 1995. 220 pp. The author's roots in all the major branches of the Religious Society of Friends are reflected in this lively, intelligent introduction to Quakerism.

*Eitzen, Ruth. *White Feather.* Herald. 64 pp. Based on the experience of a Quaker family in the settlement of Cincinnati, Ohio about 1812.

*Fager, Chuck. *Candles in the Window.* Kimo, 1991. 26 pp. A Quaker Christmas story, set in 1814 Yorkshire. Young Abram Woodhouse gains a deeper sense of his family's Quaker testimonies.

📖*Gilman, Harvey. *A Light That Is Shining: An Introduction to the Quakers.* Quaker Home Service, 1997. 101 pp. An introduction to the Quakers in Britain.

📖*Kelly, Thomas R. *A Testament of Devotion.* New York: Harper & Row, Publishers, 1941. new ed. 1992. 124 pp. This classic Quaker description of a life centered in God is a beacon of hope for each of us.

Kohler, Charles. *Grandpa Tell Us a Story.* Quaker Home Service. 95 pp. Tales of a Saxony childhood.

📖*Newman, Daisy. *A Procession of Friends.* Friends United Press, 1992. 460 pp. American Quaker history in its most readable form. The author's use of detail gives the reader a sense of place and emotion.

Quakers. Cobblestone (vol. 16, no. 10), December 1995. 48 pp. From the history magazine for young people, this issue is devoted to Friends' historical theology, biography, and socail concerns.

Quakers on the Move. Philadelphia: Friends General Conference, 1996. 150 pp. Illustrated storybook that follows generations of 10 year old Quaker children on adventures in history and service.

Some Quaker Lives

📖*Bacon, Margaret Hope. *Mothers of Feminism: The Story of Quaker Women in America.* Philadelphia: Friends General Conference, 1995. 280 pp. A thought provoking account of Quaker women who have had a strong impact on North American society.

📖*Bacon, Margaret Hope. *Valiant Friend: Lucretia Mott.* Walker, 1980. 265 pp. Definitive biography of the 19th century Quaker minister, teacher, and abolitionist.

*Bryant, Jennifer Fisher. *Lucretia Mott: A Guiding Light.* Eerdmans, 1996. 175 pp. Biography of a vital Quaker minister and social reformer.

*Fahs, Sophia Lyons, illus. by Jean R. LaRue. *George Fox: The Man Who Wouldn't . . .* Friends General Conference, 1994. 37 pp. Illustrated storybook that challenge youngsters to understand Quaker beliefs and testimonies as George Fox experienced them.

*Gormley, Beatrice. *Maria Mitchell: The Soul of an Astronomer.* Wm. B. Eerdmans, 1995. 123 pp. Biography of a Quaker woman who rose above the prejudices of her day to become America's first professional woman astronomer.

*Haskins, James. *Bayard Rustin: Behind the Scenes of the Civil Rights Movement.* Hyperion, 1997. 120 pp.

Bayard Rustin was a key player in *every* major civil rights initiative. His crowning accomplishment, the 1963 March on Washington, led to the most sweeping civil rights legislation the United States had ever seen. Age 10 and up.

Hodgkins, Violet. *A Book of Quaker Saints.* Quaker Home Service. Adventures of the early Friends told as "really good stories."

📖*Ives, Kenneth, ed. *Black Quakers: Brief Biographies.* Progresiv Publishr, 1991. 156 pp. Essays on 15 Black Quakers who have been meaningful figures in Quakersim from the 1720s to today.

📖*Lamb, Marjorie Ann (Hall). *Little Quaker Girl.* C.B.L. Services, 1989. 114 pp. A memoir of a young Friend who grew up during the 1960s in a 1910 style. Good insights into a vanished way of life.

*Sawyer, Kem Knapp. *Lucretia Mott: Friend of Justice.* Discovery Enterprises, 1992. 48 pp. Illustrated biography of this famous Quaker leader for ages 9–14.

📖*Vining, Elizabeth Gray. *Friend of Life: A Biography of Rufus M. Jones.* Philadelphia: Philadelphia Yearly Meeting, 1981. 347 pp. Account of a Friend whose ministry and writing had a profound influence on modern Quakerism.

📖*Vining, Elizabeth Gray. *Penn.* Philadelphia: Philadelphia Yearly Meeting, 1986. 298 pp. Penn's life emerges from the narrative and historical background as an inspiring story of courage, honesty, and faith.

Other Religious Traditions

*Birdseye, Debbie Holsclaw and Tom Birdseye. *What I Believe: Kids Talk About Faith*. Holiday House, 1996. 32 pp. Six students aged twelve to thirteen candidly discuss their feelings about their religious beliefs— Hindu, Buddhist, Jewish, Christian, Muslim, and Native American.

📖Rohani, M. K. *Accents of God*. One World Publications, 1991. 94 pp. Presents selections from scriptures of six world religions with brief interpretation.

*Ward, Hiley H. *My Friends' Beliefs: A Young Reader's Guide to World Religions*. Walker, 1988. 183 pp. All the major world religions, and many different ways of worshipping as a Christian, are covered in this collection of history, contemporary experience focused on a young person, and definitions.

You can find other good materials on these and other topics in your meeting library and in the Philadelphia Yearly Meeting Library. For an up-to-date listing of more books on these topics and books about Quaker Testimonies see the FGC Bookstore Catalog. For a catalog write: FGC Bookstore, 1216 Arch Street, 2B, Philadelphia, PA 19107; or call: 1-800-966-4556.